How to Draw Baby Animals

Written and illustrated by **Susan Sonkin**

Watermill Press

Baby animals are fun and easy to draw. All of
the drawings in this book are made from straight lines, curved lines,
dots, and simple shapes. Some of the shapes you will use are
circles, ovals, and sausage shapes.

Tracing is a good way to learn how to draw these shapes. Use paper
that is thin and light. Put the paper over the drawings in the book.
Trace over the basic shapes to get an idea of how big or small the
shapes should be. After you've practiced tracing the basic shapes,
you're ready to begin drawing. Just follow the easy directions, adding
to your drawing step by step.

Materials

You will not need many materials—just paper, a pencil, and an eraser.
You may also want to use crayons or markers to color your drawings.
Your baby animals will almost come to life when you color them.
Have fun with your new friends!

a baby chicken is a...
chick

A chicken egg takes three weeks to hatch. With its sharp beak, the chick pecks its way out of the egg. When the shell breaks, the chick gets its first look at the world. A few hours later, the chick will be chirping, standing, and running.

1 Baby chicks are very easy to draw. Start with a circle for the head and another bigger circle for the body. (These two circles are only to get you started. You will erase them later.)

2 Now draw two wings. Baby chicks are covered with soft, fluffy feathers. Draw little lines around the head and body for feathers. (Now erase the rough sketch lines you began with.)

3 Draw dots for the eyes and a beak that's open and chirping. Each leg is a long skinny line, and each foot is three little lines. There's your chick—*cheep, cheep!*

a baby duck is a...
duckling

Ducklings are born with soft feathers and wide-open eyes. In no time at all, they will follow their mother into the cool water. That's the nicest place to be on a hot day.

1 Start to draw your duckling with a circle. This is the head.

2 Add the body. It has a skinny neck, a round stomach, and a pointed tail. See how the body is almost the same size as the head. Ducklings have big heads. Their bodies will catch up later.

3 Now add an eye, a beak, and a wing.

4 Draw wavy lines for water. Give your duckling feathers by drawing short little lines all around the head, body, and wing. (Now you can erase the rough lines you drew before.)

Quack, quack! This duckling's ready to swim!

a baby rabbit is a...
bunny

A mother rabbit builds a nest for her babies under a tree or in tall grass. She digs a hole and lines it with grass and bits of fur. She makes a blanket from the grass and fur and tucks it over the babies when she leaves the nest.

1 Start with an oval for the head.

2 Add a circle for the body.

3 Draw long smooth ears, a round tail, small legs in front, and big round legs in the back.

4 Now add the eyes, nose, and mouth, but do it quickly—before your bunny hops away!

8

a baby cat is a...

kitten

When kittens are born, their mother licks them with her rough tongue to clean them and to help them start to breathe. The babies' eyes are shut, and their little noses cannot smell very well. They know where their mother is because they can feel her purring. After only five weeks, the kittens will be running and playing.

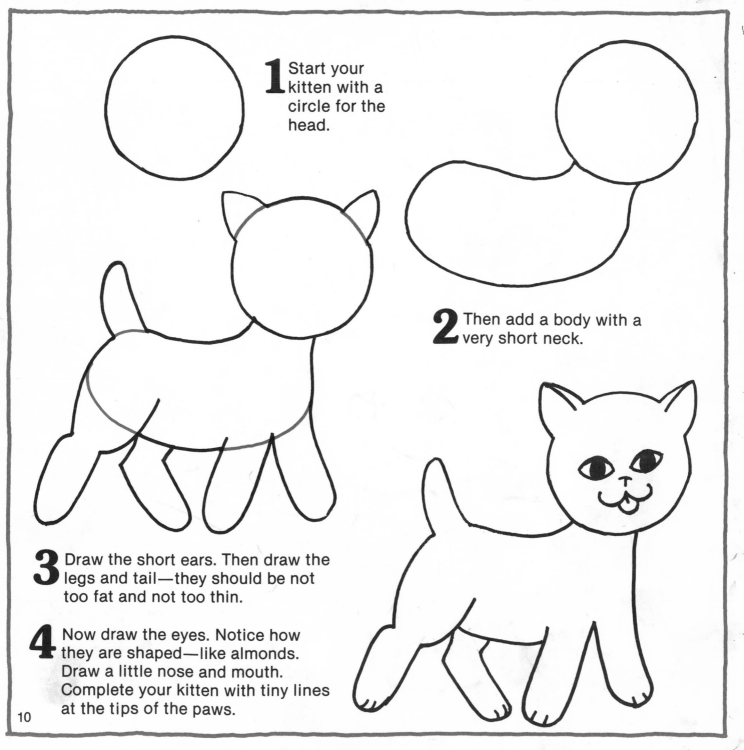

1 Start your kitten with a circle for the head.

2 Then add a body with a very short neck.

3 Draw the short ears. Then draw the legs and tail—they should be not too fat and not too thin.

4 Now draw the eyes. Notice how they are shaped—like almonds. Draw a little nose and mouth. Complete your kitten with tiny lines at the tips of the paws.

10

a baby pig is a...
piglet

Did you know that piglets are very smart animals? Pigs can learn to do anything that dogs can do: jump through hoops, dance, pull a cart, and walk a tightrope! Piglets are very special members of the farmyard.

1 Start to draw your piglet with a circle for the head.

2 Give your piglet a stubby snout and a short fat neck. The body is a fat oval.

3 Draw pointed ears. The legs are short with two pointed toes. Draw a little oval at the end of the snout for a nose and put two dots in it. Complete your piglet with a curly tail, two little eyes, and a very smart smile!

12

a baby dog is a...

puppy

A puppy will share your happy times and cheer you up when you are sad. Your little pet will play with you for hours or sit quietly at your feet. A puppy will listen to all your secrets and never tell anyone—what a good friend!

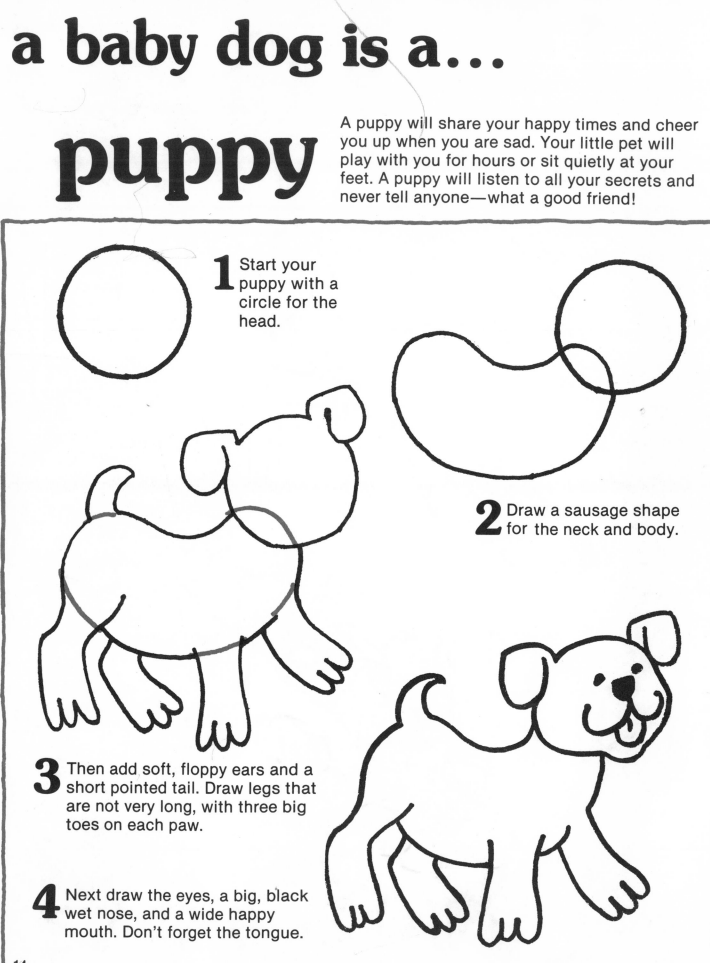

1 Start your puppy with a circle for the head.

2 Draw a sausage shape for the neck and body.

3 Then add soft, floppy ears and a short pointed tail. Draw legs that are not very long, with three big toes on each paw.

4 Next draw the eyes, a big, black wet nose, and a wide happy mouth. Don't forget the tongue.

14

a baby cow is a...

calf

When this calf is grown, she will be big and gentle and friendly. She will eat grass and grains, and she will produce lots of milk. She'll make enough milk to feed calves of her own—and you and your family, too!

1 Start your calf with a circle for the head and a short box-shaped snout.

2 Draw a wide neck. The body looks a little like a rectangle, but its corners are rounded.

3 Draw ovals for the ears. Make the legs short and strong.

4 Now draw a little line in the middle of each foot, for the calf's hoofs. Draw a long tail with some hair on the end. Add two dots for the eyes, two dots for the nose, and a mouth.

16

a baby goat is a...
kid

Baby goats love to run and play. And they are full of curiosity. They like nothing better than to explore every corner of the farmyard. Baby goats are always hungry! They may even nibble rope, wood, or a piece of cloth. These babies drink lots of milk. Milk helps them to grow big and strong.

1 Start with an oval for the head.

2 Add the neck. Draw a larger oval for the body.

3 The ears are a bit large, and the tail is small. Draw long lean legs that are good for running and playing. Add two little points to the bottom of each foot for the goat's hoofs.

4 Then add eyes, a nose, and a mischievous smile.

a baby horse is a...
foal

A foal can stand and walk an hour after it is born. This baby horse first seems unsteady on its long thin legs. But soon the foal learns to trot. Lifting its head high, the baby steps proudly along. Finally, the little horse begins to gallop— faster and faster. If it falls, it gets right up and tries again.

1 Draw a shape like a pear for the foal's head.

2 Draw a long neck and an oval for the body.

3 Add small ears to the top of the head. Make the legs long and skinny.

4 Draw short lines down the neck for the mane and a tail made from longer lines. Finish with two dots for the eyes, two dots for the nose, and a little smile.

a baby sheep is a...
lamb

This baby lamb stood on its wobbly legs soon after being born. Before long, the lamb was able to run and play in the meadow. When it is a year old, the little lamb will be grown.

1 Begin your lamb by drawing an oval for the head and two curved lines for the neck.

2 Add the body by drawing a sausage shape.

3 Now draw little ovals for the ears and a short tail. The legs are slim and not too long.

4 For the hoofs, draw a little line with a bit of fluff above it at the bottom of each foot. A squiggly line drawn all around the neck, body, and tail will make the lamb look soft and fluffy. (You can erase the rough sketch lines of your drawing now.) Add the eyes, nose, and a smile, and your lamb is ready to run and play!

22

a baby bear is a...
cub

Most bear cubs are born during the mother's winter sleep. The cubs stay in the den with their mother for about two months. When they come out of the den in the spring, they are frisky and playful. They will stay with the mother for about two years. She teaches them to hunt for food.

1 Start your cub with a circle for the head and add a short fat snout.

2 Give the cub a big round body.

3 Next, add short fat legs and a very small tail.

4 Give your bear friendly eyes, a black nose, and a little smile. Make the ears small and round. Add little lines for fur here and there.

24

a baby deer is a...
fawn

Fawns live in the woods and prairies and eat leaves, grass, and other small plants. If danger is near, they hide in the tall grass and keep very still. A fawn's coat has many spots. The spots make the fawn hard to see when it is hiding. Fawns lose their spots when they grow up.

1 Start to draw your fawn with an oval for the head.

2 Next, add a long thin neck and an oval for the body.

3 Draw little ovals for ears. Then add a tail and four long, skinny legs.

4 Add the eyes, nose, mouth, little feet, and lots of spots.

26

a baby lion is a...
cub

Young lion cubs will grow up to be big and strong like their father and mother. But before they are grown, they must learn to hunt. When they play, the cubs pretend to fight with each other—this is one way they practice their hunting skills.

1 Draw a circle for the head.

2 The body is a long sausage shape.

3 Give your lion cub a long wavy tail and short strong legs with big toes.

4 Finish with little round ears, a nose, mouth, and chin. Then add big round eyes with lines in the middle—now your lion cub can see in the dark jungle night.

28

a baby elephant is a...
calf

A newborn elephant is a very big baby! It is about three feet (1 meter) tall and weighs about two hundred pounds (90 kilograms). About one hour after being born, the baby can stand up and walk. The mother elephant protects her baby from enemies. When this baby elephant grows up, it will be the largest land animal on earth.

1 Start your baby elephant by drawing two overlapping circles. One circle is the head. The other is an ear.

2 Add another, larger circle on top of the first two circles. This is the body.

3 Add a trunk and four short, stubby legs.

4 Next, add an eye, a tail, three toenails on each foot, and an open, smiling mouth. Elephants eat leaves and small branches, so draw a jungle all around your baby elephant.